THE MORRIS OXFORD MINI-HISTORY OF OXFORD

PM

PORT MEADOW PRESS

Port Meadow Press

Oxford OX2 6HY
Registered Co. No. 4405635

ISBN 978-1-9998379-2-1

www.morrisoxford.co.uk

PORT MEADOW PRESS

If God himself on earth abode did make,
He Oxford sure would for his dwelling take.

Daniel Rogers, c.1581

The finest City in the world.

John Keats, 1817

I was a modest, good-humoured boy.
It was Oxford that has made me insufferable.

Max Beerbohm, 1899

Contents

Foreword		vi
1	Ice – and Water	1
2	First People	6
3	Romans	9
4	Saxons	14
5	Normans	20
6	Twelfth Century	23
7	Thirteenth Century	29
8	Fourteenth Century	34
9	Fifteenth Century	39
10	Sixteenth Century	44
11	Seventeenth Century	51
12	Eighteenth Century	57
13	Nineteenth Century	61
14	Twentieth Century	67
15	Twenty-First Century	72
16	Once and Future	77

Notes	80
The Origins of the University	83
A List of Oxford Colleges in Order of Foundation	89
Acknowledgements	92
About Morris Oxford	93

Foreword

IT WAS A wall plaque in Beaumont Street that did it. I remember pulling back the foliage and reading with amazement that King John and Richard the Lionheart had both been born just a few feet away from the very spot where I was standing.

Then someone in a pub told me a story about the Empress Matilda escaping from Oxford Castle on a snowy winter's night, cloaked from head to toe in white.

Then I found out that the first ever hot air balloon flight in England had taken place in a field close by ...

And so it went on. The longer I've lived in Oxford the more I've discovered; and the more I've discovered the more it seems that nearly every event of national significance has found dramatic expression in our remarkable city.

Thus was the website **Morris Oxford** born. And this *Mini-History* too.

See for yourself. You'll be amazed at what's happened here.

Onward and Oxford!

1

Ice – and Water

IN THE BEGINNING there were no rivers to ford and no oxen to ford them. There was just ice. A mile high. White and glistening. Cold and massive. Pressing down with unimaginable force.

Then, about 12,000 years ago, something happened.

The ice began to melt.

Slowly, slowly at first. Drop by drop. Until the drops began to carve tiny grooves in the surface of the ice. The grooves became rills. The rills became brooks. The brooks became streams. And the streams became rivers.

As the ice continued to melt under the warming sun, so the first sprouts of vegetation began to appear. Green shoots. Tendrils. Bits of grass.

Tiny trees.

And as the earth warmed and the grass grew, insects and small animals started to nestle in the ground. Fish multiplied in the waters, and birds began to fill the skies.

The land creaked and tipped as pressure from the mighty ice-cap was released, rising up in the north-west, sinking down in the south-east.

And the seas began to rise.

Coasts and cliffs took shape. Hilltops shrunk into islets, then slowly slipped beneath the waves. The flatlands to the east started to fill up.

A channel was formed.

An island was born.

* * *

Touch the stones of St Michael at the North Gate and you are reaching deep into ancient waters. For the vale in which our city now sits was once home to a warm, shallow sea and a reef of shimmering coral. Long, long before the ice, in a period known by geologists as the Jurassic, tiny creatures and fish of all sorts swam in its sunlit waters. When they died their myriad shells were ground together with sand and sediment, fossilised, and compressed to form what is known as Corallian limestone. The buildings of Oxford were born from this subtropical sea.

Out of these 160 million-year-old, azure waters came the rock known as 'ragstone' – rough, hard, impervious to weathering and erosion. A formidable building material, especially when sprinkled with jagged lumps of igneous granite formed from the cooling of volcanic magma many geological epochs later.

More widely visible is a variant limestone, yellower, softer, carvable and therefore easier to use for dressing buildings. Geologists have named it 'Headington Freestone', and it is the material from which much of later medieval Oxford was built. So too the royal castle at Windsor and the foundations of Eton College, some fifty miles away. Downstream. For Oxford is a place of streams and rivers. And through it runs the most important watercourse in British history – the Thames.

It is a remarkable feature of the River Thames in Oxford (or Isis[1] as some call it) that for all the surrounding geological convulsions, it has changed course very little for over fifty million years. Beyond the Chiltern Hills it originally turned north and east, entering the sea near what is now Ipswich. But in Oxford there was no such change of direction. When we stroll along the banks of Port Meadow we are following in the exact footsteps of our most ancient ancestors.

Meanwhile, Oxford's other river, the Cherwell, northernmost tributary of the Thames, curls across the midland plains from its source in Northamptonshire, encircling the University Parks as it goes until, finally, it arcs beneath Magdalen Bridge to join its bigger sibling alongside Christ Church meadows.

Between these two waters spread numerous streams, intricately interweaving, changing course with every passing century as a result of drainage, canalisation, embankment, and the vast, slow tilting of the land after the great ice-melt:

Seacourt Stream, Botley Stream, Osney Ditch, Bullstake Stream, Potts Stream, Trill Stream, Castle Mill Stream, Duke's Cut, Sheepwash Channel, Fiddler's Island Stream, Hog Acre Stream, Hinksey Stream, Eastwick Ditch, Marston Brook

Oxford is indeed a very watery place. But let's not think of this as a bad thing. Quite the opposite. The melting of the ice and the rising of the sea did not separate so much as join people together, accelerating their transport, intensifying their connectivity. Suddenly there were new neighbours to meet and new horizons to explore.

The River Thames was a conduit as much as a boundary, a liquid super-highway. As it widened and deepened so it began to support larger and larger boats, and heavier and heavier cargoes, until finally it (and they) reached the sea, and the oceans beyond.

Along its valley there were crossing points and bridges, unloading bays, wharves and fishing places. And about half-way downstream from its almost imperceptible source beneath the spreading canopy of an ash tree in Gloucestershire, at a pivotal point where the river seems to change gear, widen and accelerate, was a place where cattle could cross.

This was the oxen ford.[2]

2

First People

WHO WERE THE first island people? How do we know them?

We know them from the traces of food they left: midden piles of discarded shellfish and animal bones thrown to one side after a communal meal. We see their hand in field patterns and hedgerows and ditch-lines etched into the hillsides. We can sense their presence in the moss-covered remains of hut circles, clustered together in little settlements.

Above all, we know them for their stones. Stones which still have the power to awe and inspire us all these centuries later. Massive megaliths: standing prominent on empty hillsides; lined up in long avenues; arranged in huge, monumental circles.

The biggest stone circle of all is located in the soft chalklands fifty miles south-west of Oxford, at Avebury in Wiltshire – a giant gathering of concentric rings, the largest of which is over 300 meters in diameter, comprising 98 stones, some weighing over sixty tons, all set within an encircling ditch around nine metres deep.

The sarsen slabs of Avebury were hewn from a massive sandstone crust which covered the nearby downland, then dragged for over two miles to their current location. That's no distance, however, compared with Stonehenge, the most famous megalithic circle of all. The blue stones at its heart came from the Preseli mountains in West Wales some 200 miles away: quarried, ferried over land and sea, then shaped, smoothed, lifted, jointed and interlocked to fashion lintels as old as the pyramids of ancient Egypt.

Why were they built? Were they solar or lunar calendars? Market places? Temples? Healing centres? All of the above? Antiquarians and archaeologists have come up with many theories, usually invoking some form of 'ritual', but the fact is that no one can say for certain. What we *do* know is that these are giant monuments to Community. It took a sophisticated, integrated and co-operative culture to achieve these remarkable structures.

Oxford is home to several megalithic sites. Using lidar and aerial photography a line of hut circles and barrows can be detected stretching out to Port Meadow and beyond – the shapes of ancient human habitation traced deep into the soil. By far the most spectacular earthwork was discovered (in 2008) quite by chance, when the foundations for a new accommodation block in St John's College were being sunk. The excavation revealed the outline of an exceptionally large henge, approximately 150 metres in diameter. (By way of comparison, Stonehenge is 98 metres across.) Four thousand years old, it must have been a striking monument in its time, occupying a prime position on the raised land above the encircling waters. We can imagine people from far and wide converging there, at the very point where today's Banbury and Woodstock Roads come together to form the magisterial boulevard of St Giles, the grand entrance to Oxford from the north.

Very little of this ancient world is now visible above the surface. After a particularly dry summer the grass in the University Parks discloses the tantalising outlines of prehistoric settlement. And there is a tumulus in Port Meadow which, though denuded by centuries of rain and grazing, can still be picked out in the early morning light. Otherwise, the hallmarks of our distant ancestors have been buried and covered over by subsequent generations.

So these first people will remain forever mysterious. That's what's so fascinating about them. And it's why visitors from all over the world still marvel at the civilisation they created.

3

Romans

NO SUCH MYSTERY surrounds the Romans. They brought us their dominant language and their extraordinary engineering. They gave our island its name: Britannia. And they provided us with the first firm date in our history: 55 BC.

That was the year when Julius Caesar decided it was time to extend the boundaries of his ambition across the sea from Gaul to the mysterious island at the edge of the known world. Twice he and his men landed here. He didn't stay long – his eyes were always fixed on the prize back home in Rome – but a dramatic account of the expedition was etched for ever in his writings and in the imagination of his successors.

Nearly a century later, in the year 43, the Emperor Claudius made a more decisive landing, this time bringing enough military might to make possible a wholesale conquest. With him came battle-hardened legionaries, *ballistae* and catapults, materials for the building of fortresses and palisades, and, so the story goes, a huge war elephant from whose back he took the salute of his victorious troops at *Camulodunum* (present-day Colchester).

The Romans had come to stay. Their legions were destined to be stationed here for the next 367 years. They liked the fertile riches of the landscape near Oxford, and signs of their occupation are visible everywhere:

Roman place names – Bicester, Towcester, Dorchester – from the Latin *castrum* meaning camp.

Roman roads, straight as arrows – like Akeman Street, which crosses Oxfordshire just north of Woodstock and once linked the key towns of St Albans (*Verulamium*) and Cirencester (*Corinium*).

Roman amphitheatres – a fine example of which can be seen some thirty miles south of Oxford at Silchester (*Calleva*).

Roman villas, like those at North Leigh (a dozen miles away) and Chedworth in the Cotswolds, comfortable, affluent, decorated with fine mosaics. (At the time of writing a villa the size of Buckingham Palace has just been discovered by a metal detectorist in a field in North Oxfordshire.)

Roman underfloor heating and watering systems. In Bath (*Aquae Sulis*) you can still see the Roman plumbing which made possible this remarkable place, the warm stream from Britannia's only thermal spring gurgling out of lead pipes manufactured some two thousand years ago.

And, far to the north, you can still behold the largest, most emphatic Roman construction of all: Hadrian's Wall. For 73 miles it stretches, from coast to coast across the land, with a giant *vallum* or double-ditch some six metres deep behind it, for extra impact and security. A statement of power and subjugation in the landscape, it was designed to impress and intimidate. It still does both.

The Romans never really inhabited Oxford – not in significant numbers anyway. Only a scattering of coins have been found here over the centuries. It was probably too watery for them. They did, however, settle nearby, at Dorchester and Alchester (close to modern Bicester), and their presence had a notable impact on the development of Oxford in two respects.

First, they made it a centre for their pottery industry – one of the biggest and most important on the whole island of Britannia – to the extent that many ceramic artefacts are now collectively known by archaeologists as 'Oxford-ware'. Here were produced innumerable pots to be crammed with foodstuffs, flagons to be filled with wine, *mortaria* for the grinding of grains, and all manner of plates, platters, jugs, beakers and bowls. At least two dozen kilns have been excavated in the Headington area, where the local clays and plentiful wood provided ideal baking materials. This was pottery manufacturing on a vast scale, evidence of an industry which thrived for at least two centuries (*c*.200–400).

More enduringly, the Romans imposed their stone foundations on the great North-South thoroughfare that defines Oxford. Sitting atop a gravel terrace deposited by the meltwaters of the ice age, the Woodstock Road carves its way straight into the centre of the town, making for the highest point, Carfax,[3] then dropping down via St Aldates to the all-important river crossing and beyond.

But *festina lente*! Lest we march along too hastily in our Roman desire to get ahead, let us briefly return to Headington hill and take a moment to pause and reflect. For here, in the 1970s, in the grounds of the old Churchill Hospital, on the site of one of the biggest concentrations of Roman kilns, was found a baked clay shard on which were inscribed these words:

Tamesubugus fecit
'Thames-dweller' made this

Is this the first-named denizen of Oxford? We can't be sure. Who knows what discoveries lie in store as we dig further back in time? But it is exciting to think of someone settling and making their mark here, on the side of a pot, in a place where writing was destined to become so important.

4

Saxons

IF CONVENTIONAL HISTORIES were anything to go by the next phase of Oxford's history would be difficult to discern, for the simple reason that we would all have been plunged into darkness. According to some of the more lurid accounts, when the last Roman legionaries sailed away from our shores in the year 410 they switched the lights off and a shadow fell across the land.

The Dark Ages.

There seems little doubt that the post-Roman period was one of increased instability and insecurity, with the constant threat of incursion from overseas. But there were also moments of intense illumination. The Lindisfarne gospels – some of the most beautiful artefacts ever created – were made during this time, lovingly pored over by the monks of that island abbey. With quill feathers and sharpened reeds they scribed their sacred words and images onto parchment and vellum: inks of red vermillion, saffron yellow, verdigris and lapis lazuli blue (from the far-away land we now know as Afghanistan). Burnished with gold leaf and silver, these were works of luminous beauty, sophistication and, above all, devotion.

For this was a period of a great religious awakening in Britain, an age of saints: Columba (521–597) in Iona; David (500–589) in Wales; Augustine (d.604) in Canterbury; Cuthbert (634–687) in Lindisfarne; and many other holy men and women, including our very own Frideswide (c.650–727).

Frideswide (or Frithuswith: her distinctive name means 'peace' and 'strong') is an interesting saint, not simply because she is female; and her association with Oxford is very specific. Versions of her story are recorded in two medieval manuscripts. They tell of her noble upbringing, her beauty, her virtue and her determination to become a nun. They also relate how she was pursued by a Mercian King, Algar, who desired to make her his wife. She declined his advances and moved to a hide-out in woods beyond the tiny hamlet of Binsey. The rapacious Algar refused to be deterred, and eventually discovered Frideswide's secret location. But, just as he was about to ride out in hot pursuit, a miracle occurred: Algar was struck blind! Ever compassionate, Frideswide restored his sight – and later that of others who came to visit her – using the waters of a holy well which she had magicked into existence (the 'Treacle Well' made famous many lifetimes later by Lewis Carroll).

Eventually it was safe for Frideswide to return to Oxford. There she achieved her life-long goal of establishing a priory. Cult status followed swiftly. When she died, on 19 October 727, her grave became a pilgrimage shrine. From this moment on, Oxford's reputation as a tourist destination was guaranteed.

The choice of setting for Frideswide's priory was significant: on prime land, high up and overlooking the river crossing – a very important spot symbolically and strategically. It was no accident that, nearly a thousand years later, first Cardinal Wolsey and then King Henry VIII chose the same location on which to site their church, college and, in due course, cathedral.

Post-Roman Oxford was already an important place, and as the decades passed it was destined to become ever more so. The town's defences, which originally had been made of compacted earth topped with a wooden palisade, were transformed into stone walls. Towers were established at the four entrances: St Michael at the North Gate stands to this day. By the ninth century Oxford had been officially designated a *burh* (a defensible settlement or fortified enclave) in confirmation of its size, significance and status.

King Alfred the Great (848–899) is said to have

been responsible for organising Oxford's layout, the streets set in a characteristic Saxon grid, with narrow strips running at right-angles off the main roads.[4] The town is in many ways a symbol of his reign. For it was a key settlement on the frontline of Wessex, the kingdom he triumphantly defended against the next wave of would-be invaders – the Danes. After years of bloody conflict Alfred decisively defeated the Great Heathen Army at the battle of Edington in 878, whereupon their leader, Guthrum, sued for peace, converted to Christianity, and swore fealty to his Saxon overlord.

Alfred secured his territory through military and naval prowess. But it was his powers of organisation as much as his warrior skills which earned him the sobriquet unique among British monarchs, 'the Great'. Having established the primacy of Wessex by arms, he safeguarded its future through a number of far-sighted legal, fiscal and administrative reforms, based on the establishment of shires as the key unit of regional organisation. He also placed great emphasis on education, scholarship and literacy and was reputed to spend hours translating the bible long into the night. It is even claimed that he invented the 'candle clock' as a way of managing his time more effectively, an example of enlightened diligence from which Oxford students might, to this day, derive inspiration. (*Dominus Illuminatio Mea* is the university motto.)

King Alfred was a local man, born in Wantage fifteen miles away. When, in 1693, the so-called Alfred Jewel was discovered in the marshes of Athelney in Somerset (where he had taken refuge during the tumultuous early years of his reign) it was only right that it should have been bequeathed to the Ashmolean museum. An exquisite example of Saxon craftsmanship, and a memento of his continuing presence, the inscription around its filigree setting reads *Aelfred mec heht gewyrcan*: 'Alfred had me made.' It is a fitting epithet for Oxford too.

* * *

There is bound to have been some intermingling between Saxons and Danes in the century following Alfred's death, especially in a busy trading town such as Oxford, close to the border between Saxon Wessex and the land to the east known as the Danelaw;[5] but it cannot always have been an easy accommodation. 'Sprouting up like weeds among the wheat,' was how one Saxon commentator described his foreign-born neighbours.

A recent archaeological discovery provides evidence of one particularly grim episode in their relations. St Brice's Day, 13 November, was the traditional occasion of a feast celebrating the ritual slaughter of livestock. In the year 1002 it marked a human massacre. Across the kingdom the indigenous population rose up in bloody insurgence. In Oxford, the vastly outnumbered Danes sought sanctuary in St Frideswide's church. It was torched, and they were burnt to a cinder. An excavation in the grounds of St John's College in 2008 revealed a grave-pit containing the mangled skeletons of nearly forty young Viking men, their charred bones hacked and mutilated. There are doubtless more bodies that have not yet come to light.

The Danish response was swift and equally murderous. King Sweyn Forkbeard, whose sister Gunnhild was among those killed, dispatched a fearsome army across the North Sea and bloody vengeance was exacted. Oxford was laid to waste (1009) and the Saxon king Aethelred, who had commanded the St Brice's Day uprising, was forced to flee abroad. He returned, however, after Sweyn's death, and it was one of Aethelred's sons, Edward the Confessor (born in Islip, seven miles from Oxford) who eventually became the last-but-one King of Wessex and England.[6]

5

Normans

THE FINAL WAVE of invasion was the bloodiest and most dramatic of all – and it was to prove decisive.

Historians like to remind us that the Normans were Norsemen, so we might perhaps think of William the Conqueror as the ultimate Viking overlord (even if his family's Scandinavian roots had been sunk in Gallic soil for many generations.) It was the Normans, more than any previous invaders, who shaped this island, and bequeathed us the best-known date in our history: 1066.

The Conqueror was crowned at Westminster on Christmas Day of that momentous year, and the process of intensive subjugation began more or less immediately. Not for King William an accommodation with the locals. He rapidly and systematically killed or removed the English nobility, replacing them with his own henchmen, parcelling up the land and handing out the spoils to those who had fought by his side at the Battle of Hastings.

Then he set about establishing his dominion in stone. Dozens of castles were built over the course of the next two decades, rock-like projections of Norman power. Most famous is the great square keep known as the White Tower, which stands at the heart of the Tower of London. But there were many other massive examples established around the country – notably at Chepstow on the Welsh border and on the cliffs of Dover guarding the crossing to Normandy. And at fifteen sites across the country – from Durham to Chichester, from Norwich to Hereford – thousands of men laboured to construct immense cathedrals that would dazzle and awe the subjugated locals.

William's henchman in Oxford was Robert d'Oilly. He, too, had building ambitions. Overlooking the western crossing of the river, on a giant mound or *motte* over fifty feet high and five times as wide, he ordered the construction of Oxford Castle, its heavy ragstone walls punctuated by watchtowers, set above a freshly dug moat. Within the safety of the bailey precinct, adjoining the great (still standing) tower of St George,[7] he built a chapel (1074), whose priests were to play an important role in the later emergence of the University. Only the crypt now remains. Its squat columns and low, subterranean arches convey a feeling of oppression: thick-set, rough-hewn and powerful, not unlike the Conqueror himself. The carving on the pillars is basic: the distinctive zigzag chevron ornamentation (visible around the church and chancel archways of Headington, Iffley, Holywell, St Peter-in-the-East, and especially St Frideswide's) was to come later, once the conquest had been consolidated. Meanwhile, the Domesday book (1086) records over five hundred domestic houses within Oxford's town walls as 'waste', suggesting either wanton destruction or wholesale abandonment as a result of sudden, almost certainly violent, changes in landholding.

On the south side of the town Robert d'Oilly commissioned one of the most remarkable constructions in the entire kingdom – a massive stone causeway, three carriages wide and stretching nearly half a mile across the marshlands towards Abingdon, with perhaps as many as forty arches. Grandpont. Great Bridge. The name says it all.

Parts of it remain to this day, its ancient blocks undergirding the modern bridge. Nearly a thousand years later, you get a sense of how strategically important Oxford had become: the prime crossing from Northampton to Southampton; the meeting of the rivers Cherwell and Thames; a confluence and a gateway; the shaper of Oxford's destiny. There had been some kind of fording place here for a long time, but it was the Normans who fixed it for ever in stone.

6

Twelfth Century

IN THE CENTURY that followed, Oxford Castle had two particularly important residents. The first of them shall remain secret until the end of this book. The second was none other than Matilda, wife of the Holy Roman Emperor and daughter of King Henry I of England.

Matilda had been forced to retreat here in an attempt to escape the clutches of her cousin and civil-war rival for the throne, King Stephen. When his forces besieged Oxford castle they seemed to have her trapped. The great central tower has long since disappeared, but we can imagine Matilda gazing out over its battlements towards the enemy soldiers encircling her, and the open fields beyond.

Snow fell heavily throughout that winter of 1142. One shimmering, frosty night, the Empress, cloaked from head to toe in white, managed to slip silently and unnoticed in her disguise out of the castle. The medieval chronicler, Henry of Huntingdon, records how she 'trick(ed) the eyes of the besiegers by her white clothes in the dazzle of the snow' and made her way 'across the frozen Thames', first to Wallingford, then over the sea to France – and safety.

Matilda never returned to England. She was laid to rest in Normandy a quarter of a century after her great escape. But her spirit lives on in the annals of Oxford history. And her blood too. For it was *her* son who triumphantly ascended the throne in 1154, when Stephen eventually died.

King Henry II is best known for one of the most shocking events in British history: the murder in Canterbury Cathedral of Archbishop Thomas Becket. When news of the atrocity came out, everyone – the entire nation not just the monastic community – was shocked, horrified and outraged. Henry realised the terrible truth of what had been done. He prayed to God for forgiveness. He wrote to the Pope to apologise. And, as a final act of penance, to show he was sincere in his regret, he entered Canterbury Cathedral barefoot, dressed in sack cloth and covered in ashes.

The King had been humiliated. What's more he had made a major tactical blunder. For, if the aim of Becket's assassination was to establish royal priority in matters ecclesiastical, it backfired spectacularly. Thomas might have lost his life, but the Church had got what it sought. Its independence from state control was secured for a further four centuries. The Pope saw his opportunity and was quick to capitalise. Thomas was rapidly canonised as a Christian martyr and a lavish shrine built in his honour. Overnight it became the most important pilgrimage site in the land.

In his *Canterbury Tales*, written two centuries later, Geoffrey Chaucer paints a vivid portrait of the motley group who gather at the Tabard Inn, Southwark, before setting out together on their pilgrim journey. One of them is a 'Clerk from Oxenford', whom he depicts as thin, impoverished, hard-working and deeply studious.

> Yet hadde he but litel gold in cofre;
> But al that he myghte of his freendes hente,
> On books and on lernynge he it spente.

There is good evidence that Chaucer was familiar with Oxford: he chose it as the setting for one of his best-known pilgrim stories, 'The Miller's Tale', in which he displays signs of detailed local knowledge.[8] Whether or not he actually lived here for a significant length of time we don't know and probably never will. The point is that, by the time Chaucer penned his poem at the end of the fourteenth century, Oxford had clearly established itself in the popular imagination as a centre of learning.

Why here? Why Oxford? Perhaps because of its geographical position in the middle of the country, at what the All Souls historian A.L. Rowse calls a 'crossroads of cultures' with 'significant Celtic associations, fertilising in their effects'.[9] (Rowse was Cornish.) Perhaps because of the influence of St Frideswide's scholarly prior, Robert of Cricklade (*c.*1100–1174) whose work encapsulated the latest scientific knowledge of the day.[10] Perhaps because of the Chapel of St George, safely located within the walls of Oxford Castle, which provided a focal point for a group of erudite teaching canons under a succession of ambitious archdeacons.[11] Perhaps because of the various monastic orders who chose to set up Houses in Oxford – the Dominicans (who established themselves here in 1221), Franciscans (1224), Carmelites (1266) and Augustinians (1267).

Whatever the reason (probably a mixture of all the above) Oxford's reputation as a centre of intellectual enquiry grew steadily throughout the course of the twelfth century. The royal clerk, archdeacon and historian Gerald of Wales was invited to lecture here in 1188. Other eminent academic visitors followed. Oxford began to attract teachers ('masters') who in turn attracted pupils ('scholars') to study Canon and

Roman Law, Arts and Theology. With every passing year Oxford drew in more and more aspiring students from all over the kingdom. (For more detail about the origins and early development of the university see the Appendix, pp.83–88.)

This was the world Chaucer was referencing at the end of the fourteenth century, a world in which Oxford and scholarship had already become synonymous in the public mind.

But let us return briefly to King Henry II, for, notwithstanding his murderous rage, he shaped Oxford in two specific and very important ways.

First, in 1167 he issued a decree banning home-grown scholars from crossing the Channel to study at Paris, at that time Europe's pre-eminent university. This was to prove decisive in protecting, consolidating and accelerating Oxford's intellectual reputation and growth.

Second, Henry accorded Oxford a royal charter granting its merchants and citizens certain special privileges and exemptions, 'liberties, customs, laws and immunities'. These put the town on a par with London, thereby securing it a special position within the kingdom.

A very particular honour accorded to the Mayor of Oxford (which lapsed only in 1831) seems to bear out this privileged status: the right to serve the monarch at the coronation banquet. Only three mayors in the entire kingdom had similar rights – the Lord Mayor of London who (along with his Oxford counterpart) assisted the Chief Butler, and the Mayor of Winchester who assisted the King's Cook.

In matters of state Oxford clearly held an important place in Henry's thinking. It also held a special place in the affairs of his royal heart. He visited often and loved nothing better than to hunt in the grounds of nearby Woodstock Palace. Deer were not the king's only quarry, for he found himself smitten by a local beauty, Rosamund 'The Fair' Clifford, whom he pursued with equal ardour and dedication.

Henry's formidable wife, Queen Eleanor of Aquitaine, quickly tired of her husband's infatuation. She insisted that he end his dalliance, and commanded that his young mistress be removed to a nunnery. Rosamund was duly despatched to the recently established convent at Godstow, a safe distance beyond Oxford's city walls. She died there shortly afterwards in mysterious circumstances (poisoning is suspected).

Ah, Rosamund. Fair Rosamund. Another royal friendship destined to end in tragedy. These were indeed difficult times in which to befriend a hot-blooded king.

7

Thirteenth Century

It is a remarkable fact that two future kings of England were born in Oxford. Remarkable too that nothing remains of the building in which they came into the world. All that can be seen is a plaque bearing this inscription:

NEAR TO THIS SITE
STOOD THE KING'S HOUSES
LATER KNOWN AS
BEAUMONT PALACE

KING RICHARD I
WAS BORN HERE IN 1157
AND KING JOHN IN 1167

Richard and John. Lionheart and Lackland. Two of our nation's most notorious monarchs. Brothers of a very different kind – the former devoted to the idea of a crusade to recapture Jerusalem from the Muslim armies of Saladin; the latter hopelessly failing to assert monarchical authority at home in the face of ever-increasing pressure from the barons.

The Lionheart story is, on the face of it, a simple one to relate. Richard was an out-and-out warrior. He liked nothing better than being on military manoeuvres, and it was no surprise when he eventually met his death via a crossbow bolt. Critics point out that he spent under a hundred days of his ten-year reign in the land of his birth, and that he came close to bankrupting the country in pursuit of his grand ambition – but in most history books Richard embodies all that was fine and heroic about medieval kingship. A statue of him stands today on a granite plinth outside the Palace of Westminster. Sword aloft, bestriding a mighty charger, he is the very essence of chivalric virtue and courage.

There are no such grand statues of King John. He remains forever consigned to the shadows of history as the sly and incompetent ruler who tried to usurp his older brother, who lost the crown jewels in the Wash, and who, above all, was humiliatingly forced by the barons to affix his royal seal to the Magna Carta at Runnymede in 1215.

The Bodleian Library contains no fewer than four (out of a world total of seventeen) copies of the pre-1300 Magna Carta. And Oxford was the setting for the most significant episode in the history of monarchical-baronial relations. For it was here that their leader, Simon de Montfort, Earl of Leicester, forced John's successor, the boy king Henry III, to endorse a set of agreements designed to build on the Great Charter of Liberties, in which was stated:

> No free man shall be seized or imprisoned, or stripped of his rights or possessions, or outlawed or exiled. Nor will we proceed with force against him except by the lawful judgement of his peers or by the law of the land. To no one will we sell, to no one deny or delay right or justice.

The Provisions of Oxford, formally approved in 1258, set out further limits to the powers of the king and established a partially elected council to advise him. Also mooted by de Montfort was the idea of convening, three times a year, an assembly comprising two representatives from every shire in the land, to discuss not just the raising of finance but matters of state more generally. Oxford, it might be argued, was home to this country's first ever written constitution and first ever elected *parlement*.

The experiment in consensus and consultation was short-lived.[12] When the pious and malleable Henry was succeeded by his warrior-like son things fast became very different.

Edward I was a giant of a man, well over six feet in

height, and as ambitious, aggressive and determined as he was tall. Moreover, he had been on crusade and was battle-hardened. When he ascended to the throne in 1272 he was in no mood to compromise or accede to the Provisions of Oxford. His mission was simple: to reassert his supreme and unquestioned regal authority throughout the entire land.

Having already killed de Montfort at the battle of Evesham (1265) he proceeded to crush the Welsh Prince Llewelyn, whose heartland in Snowdonia he encircled with a ring of mighty castles. The finest of these was at Caernarfon, and it was there in 1284 that he committed the ultimate act of royal imposition, raising aloft his new-born son and declaring him Prince of Wales. Finally, he turned his gaze to the north. He confiscated the Stone of Destiny from Scone Castle and removed it to Westminster, then spent the remaining years of his reign trying to hammer the Scots into submission.

Edward's vision was of an island empire, unified under the undisputed overlordship of the King of England. Had it not been for the incompetence of his feckless son, Edward II, this might have come to pass. But it was not to be. Oxford's fourth college, Exeter, was founded in the same year, 1314, that Robert the Bruce humiliated the English army at Bannockburn; and the fifth college, Oriel, opened its doors just a few months before Edward met his death in 1327, assassinated in grisly and ignominious fashion at Berkeley Castle.

8

Fourteenth Century

TALKING OF GRUESOME death, the fourteenth century was dominated by mortality on a vast, searing and unprecedented scale. Between the years 1347 and 1349 Britain, along with the whole continent of Europe, suffered the most devastating pandemic in human history: the Black Death.

Over fifty million people perished – between a quarter and half of the entire population of Europe. Devastation on such a scale is almost unimaginable. By way of comparison, deaths in World War Two (military and civilian combined) are estimated to account for less than five per cent of world population.

The symptoms of the contagion were hideous to behold – black boils or *buboes* (hence the term bubonic plague) clustered around the lymph nodes in the neck, armpit and groin. A terrible fever, sweating, sickness and diarrhoea ensued. Death followed swiftly and almost inevitably.

Many communities ran out of people to dig pits

and bury the bodies, leaving piles of blackened corpses to fester, rot and in turn promote more plague. Whole swathes of the country were ravaged to vanishing point. Ordnance Survey maps are still peppered with signs for 'deserted villages' dating from this period.

The more densely populated the settlement the quicker the plague spread. Oxford already had a reputation as a hotbed of 'foul Disease ... said to have been contracted almost in an Epidemical Manner'[13] as a result of prostitution and undergraduate excess. But the Black Death was of an altogether different order.

Some scholars of the University and wealthier townsmen were able to escape to houses in the country where they waited until winter time before returning (plague thrived in warmer weather). But for those unable to get away, the conditions were appalling.

It took over two hundred years for the population of Britain to return to pre-Black Death levels. Every aspect of life was shaped by it, and many parts of the country never recovered. For the minority who managed to survive, however, there were silver linings even to this darkest of episodes. Given the scarcity of manpower this was one of the few times in history when agricultural labourers and peasants were able to demand improved conditions and wages. In fact, in 1381, their demands culminated in a wholesale Peasants' Revolt.

There were more than occasional riots in Oxford too, but for different reasons. The town was full of boisterous young men away from home. Student existence was, in the words of one historian, 'riotously unregulated'.[14] 'Chronic indiscipline' was the order of the day.[15] To the rivalry between faculties and between monastic houses, was added the often violent feuding between different colleges and hostels. Local patriotisms were fiercely asserted, depending on whether the lodgings were occupied by Welsh, Irish or Scots. Worse still was the antagonism between the Englishmen from north or south of the River Nene (they even referred to themselves as two 'nations'). And when they weren't all brawling among themselves, they found frequent opportunities to test their mettle against the people of Oxford ('town v. gown'). The widespread availability of alcohol and blunt instruments didn't help.

Riots broke out frequently, several of them lethal and widespread. One such outrage in 1209 culminated in the death of a townswoman and the lynching of three innocent scholars in retribution. A sizeable group of students, fearing for their lives, led an exodus from Oxford to set up an alternative scholarly community in the Fens. Thus was born the University of Cambridge.

The following century, in 1333, there was talk of setting up a third university at Stamford[16] in Lincolnshire, but this was suppressed by special pleading to the King – thereby ensuring the Oxbridge duopoly which went on to dominate English higher education for the next five hundred years.

On another occasion, when a Papal Legate was despatched to Oxford to try to improve the morals of the students, one thing led to another and his servant ended up being shot dead by an undergraduate armed with a bow and arrow. Scarcely a month went by without the accounts of the town bailiffs and university proctors, who attempted to police the streets, recording some violent injury. In the words of one historian:

> There is probably not a single yard of ground in any part of the classic High Street that lies between St Martin's and St Mary's which has not, at one time or another, been stained with blood. There are historic battlefields on which less has been spilt.[17]

The greatest 'affray' started on Tuesday 10 February 1355: the feast of St Scholastica. It was to last three days and leave a dreadful toll of death and destruction. The tinder was sparked by a dispute in the Swindlestock Tavern, close to the centre of town, on the corner of what is now Queen Street and St Aldate's. Two students, Walter Spryngeheuse and Roger de Chesterfield, complained to the landlord, John Croidon, about the price and poor quality of his liquor. Insults were exchanged, then blows, then people piled in from all sides. The bells of St Martin's and St Mary's rang out summoning reinforcements from town and university. A riot ensued.

Three days later 30 townspeople and 63 students lay dead (one of them supposedly scalped), and smoke rose from dozens of torched and ransacked buildings. Only the presence of royal forces, despatched from Woodstock, eventually managed to quell the violence. When order was finally restored and the King had made his judgment upon the affair, the Town Mayor was forced to apologise to the University Chancellor. More than that, he and his civic officers were required to do public penance, swear on oath to honour the University's privileges, and pay recompense of a penny per head for every student killed.

His mayoral successors had to do the same, in an annual church service of humiliating remembrance which lasted nearly 500 years, ceasing only in 1825. Memories take a long time to fade in Oxford.

9

Fifteenth Century

ONE UNFORESEEN CONSEQUENCE of the Black Death was a revolution in farming.

The scarcity of people to cultivate the land left more space for animals to roam – sheep in particular. Their fleeces were valuable. Once washed, carded and spun they could be made into wool and woven into fine tapestries. Southern Britain, with its gently rolling hills and lush pastures, was perfect sheep country, and a rich trade in wool and cloth developed, with the Cotswolds, west of Oxford, at its heart.

Several of the colleges derived considerable wealth from their landholdings beyond the city. The coarser wool was processed locally (a substantial broadcloth and, later, blanket industry grew up in Witney, for example) while the higher quality fleeces were exported to the Lowlands of Europe where they were woven into luxury wall-hangings of considerable refinement and value.

The balance between town and gown tipped. The

University became ever more affluent, while the city traders struggled to come to terms with the depredations wrought by the Black Death. The collapse of property prices in Oxford at this time accentuated this process by providing an opportunity for the colleges to acquire more land within the city walls to fuel their expansion.

It was while trading in Flanders that a merchant by the name of William Caxton first caught sight of a machine that was to change the future of Oxford, Britain and the world: the printing press. Back home in Westminster, Caxton decided to set up a new business. In 1476 he produced England's first printed book: an edition of Chaucer's *Canterbury Tales*. Oxford wasn't far behind London. The first book was printed here in 1478, a privately commissioned *Exposition of the Apostolic Creed* (a copy of which is still held by the Bodleian Library).

A few years later, in 1484, Caxton brought out another printed volume: *The Book of the Knight in the Tower*. Its title echoes a headline of the time, one which has fascinated people ever since – the mystery of the Princes in the Tower, taken into custody for their 'protection and safe-keeping' at the behest of their uncle, King Richard III ... and never to be seen again.

It reminds us that the fifteenth century, like its

predecessors, was shaped by yet more violence and internecine rivalry – the so-called Wars of the Roses, a dynastic conflict between the houses of York and Lancaster which began with the deposition and death of Richard II in 1399 and only ended with the slaying of his royal namesake at Bosworth in 1485.

This was the century of the Henrys: starting with the coronation of Henry IV and closing with Henry VII on the throne. Henry V, 'the warlike Harry', was a student at The Queen's College, Oxford (founded 1341) before turning his sights across the Channel; and it was his son, Henry VI, who co-founded All Soul's College in 1438 to pray for the eternal life of his father and 'All the Dukes, Earls, Barons, Knights, Esquires and others who fell in the war for the crown of France'.

All Souls was the ninth Oxford college to be founded, eleven years after Lincoln (1427) and two decades before Magdalen (1458). These are three of Oxford's finest colleges, each distinctive in a very different way: Lincoln for the special intimacy of its proportions, giving it, according to Nikolaus Pevsner, 'more of the character of a fifteenth century college than any other in Oxford'; Magdalen for its grand cloisters and ante-chapel, expansive parkland (and, later, bell-tower); All Souls for its continuous status, unique among Oxbridge colleges, as a home for senior academics rather than undergraduates.

By the fifteenth century the idea of what constituted a college had become established, and it was during this period that, according to Oxford's leading architectural historian Geoffrey Tyack, 'the colleges made their decisive architectural impact on the urban fabric of Oxford'.[18]

The pattern had been set a few decades earlier, by New College, the seventh college to be founded (1379). Its originator was William of Wykeham, Bishop of Winchester, Lord Chancellor, and Clerk of the King's Building Works. 'An ecclesiastical grandee of the first order', with architectural ambitions to match,[19] Wykeham defined for the first time the key components of what is now considered to be the classic college lay-out: a chapel and common refectory area/dining hall (reflecting the university's medieval monastic origins) a library, master's lodge, garden, and accommodation arranged around a quadrangular (sometimes cloistered) courtyard.

It was a younger brother of Henry V (who had fought alongside him at Agincourt) after whom Oxford's first bespoke reading room was named. Upon his death in 1447 Humfrey, Duke of Gloucester, donated no fewer than 281 volumes, a remarkable quantity of books at a time when the entire university collection numbered only twenty.

Above the newly built Divinity Room with its

magnificent fan vaulting, a library was established (1489) in his memory. From this moment on Oxford became a mecca not just for scholars but also bibliophiles, with Humfrey's room of painted panels, elaborate ceilings and finely carved oak bookcases at its heart.

The Bodleian Library, which grew up around the Duke Humfrey collection, now contains over thirteen *million* written items, including the so-called Gutenberg Bible, the first Latin bible to be produced (in 1455) using a moveable metal font and special, oil-based inks – the (literal) prototype of all printed publications.

Not surprisingly a book trade began to flourish in Oxford, and a thriving printing industry too. Oxford University Press (founded in 1586) is the world's largest university publishing house, producing 6,000 new titles every year, with offices in 52 countries and a global turnover in excess of £800m. The pen had always been mightier than the sword as far as Oxford was concerned. The printed word was to prove even more powerful.

10

Sixteenth Century

'IN THE BEGINNING was the Word.' Thus states the Bible. The sixteenth century was dominated by a series of terrible disputes about holy words. The holier they were the more they were contested; and the more they were contested the more blood was shed.

Martin Luther sparked a Reformation in Germany, with language, scripture, translation and biblical interpretation at its theological heart. In Switzerland, John Calvin's *Institutes of the Christian Religion* inspired the production of the so-called Geneva Bible in 1560, its commentarial margin notes infused with criticism of the religious status quo. All across Europe voices were raised in protest at the overweening and corrupt power of priests, the papacy, and ultimately the structure and practices of the entire Roman Catholic church.

In Britain the argument was intensified (and complicated) by the events surrounding Henry VIII's divorce from Queen Catherine of Aragon in 1533. The Pope refused to sanction it. Henry refused to remain married to her. What followed was the notorious 'Break with Rome', the establishment of the Church of England with Henry as its Head, and the dissolution of the monasteries: in short, a convulsive change to the structure of authority in Tudor England.

The physical effect of Henry's reign in Oxford, as in so many other parts of his realm, was dramatic. The monastic houses of the Austin Friars, the Franciscans, Dominicans and Carmelites were rapidly closed. So too the exclusively monastic colleges – Gloucester, Durham, Canterbury, St Bernard's and St Mary's, whose memories now survive only in street names. Finally, Henry's commissioners turned their eyes on Oxford's three abbeys – Rewley, Godstow and Osney. Their roofs were de-leaded, their stained glass removed, their shrines dismantled, their treasures looted, and their destruction secured.

The dissolution of Osney Abbey was particularly shocking, for it was the biggest building in Oxford (bigger even than the castle it faced across the river) and had been Oxford's mother church for centuries. In 1546 Henry VIII confiscated its lands and assets in order to re-endow the college Cardinal Wolsey had founded on the historic site of St Frideswide's priory. This Henry renamed and refounded as Christ Church which he designated as the new centre of religious focus in Oxford. That is why we have the strange (indeed unique) phenomenon of one of the smallest cathedrals in Britain located within the walls of an academic institution and doubling up as a college chapel.

The effect of the Reformation and the dissolution of the monasteries went far beyond the physical environment. It was nothing less than a spiritual, philosophical, psychological, personal, and political trauma. A.L. Rowse calls these 'the ulcerated middle decades', when 'with chops and changes, hangings and burnings, the hopes of humanism, of rational and moderate reform, became submerged'.[20]

For the remainder of the century, bitter rivalry between competing religious affiliations and allegiances dominated public discourse. Claims and counterclaims of heresy and orthodoxy proliferated (and were much amplified in this new era of printing) often with venomous and destructive consequences.

Oxford, then as now, was a place where words were scrutinised with special care, so it comes as little surprise to find it at the heart of feverish religious controversy. Two of England's foremost biblical translators were Oxford scholars. In the fourteenth century John Wycliffe, a former master of Balliol College, had translated the 'vulgate' (Latin) Bible into vernacular English and been accused of heresy as a result. Wycliffe's literary successor, William Tyndale, (for several years a scholar at Magdalen Hall, which later became Hertford College) was similarly accused, for translating the Hebrew and Greek versions of the bible in ways deemed subversive by the Church authorities. Unlike Wycliffe, however, who lived out his days in the quiet of the East Midlands countryside, Tyndale was hunted down in Antwerp and executed, in 1536 (just months after Anne Boleyn lost her head).

Debate raged. The balance of power shifted to and fro. Henry was briefly succeeded by his son Edward VI, whose court was Protestant in inclination. But his reign was short-lived (1547–53) and he was followed onto the throne by his half-sister Mary. The daughter of Catherine of Aragon, her allegiance was, not surprisingly, to the Catholic cause. It was Queen 'Bloody' Mary who, in the years 1555–56 ordered the burning at the stake of the 'Oxford Martyrs', Hugh Latimer, Nicholas Ridley and none other than Archbishop Thomas Cranmer, once the most powerful prelate in the land. The great oak door of Balliol College is said to have buckled and blistered, such was the intensity of the heat from the pyre. The precise spot where they perished in Broad Street, on the site of the medieval cattle market, is now marked by a cross in the road.

Under the long reign of Queen Elizabeth I (1558–1603) a Protestant settlement was eventually established, and with it a glorious resurgence of creativity in drama and literature; but not without further persecution and bloodshed – including the execution in 1581 of the Roman Catholic Edmund Campion (after whom Campion Hall is named) at Tyburn and, in Oxford eight years later, of George Nichols, Richard Yaxley, Thomas Belson and Humphrey Prichard at a site in Holywell Street now marked by a small and easily missed blue plaque.

These were tempestuous times indeed – and not just on the home front. For this was also the period when, having fought off the threat of invasion by the Spanish Armada in 1588, English ships began an informal maritime offensive which was to reshape the map of the world. Their captains were the stuff of legend. Prior to his game of bowls on Plymouth Hoe, Francis Drake, circumnavigated the globe in *The Golden Hinde* (1577–80), while another nautical knight, Walter Raleigh (1552–1618), not only introduced tobacco and potatoes to these shores, but also found time to compose poetry and commence work on a 'historie of the worlde'. These were pioneering days in the history of exploration and discovery, an age which saw the beginnings of overseas expansion on an unprecedented scale.[21]

Small wonder, then, that when William Shakespeare came to build a theatre on the banks of the River Thames he called it The Globe. Britain was turning from an inconsequential island off the edge of a continent into the hub of an international, ocean-going Empire. The world was in the process of being encompassed.

It is fitting to end this chapter with reference to the Bard. 'Soule of the age', 'myriad-minded', Shakespeare borrowed many words and phrases from the Bible – and he contributed many more of his own. The consummate man of words, he understood all too well their power to provoke complicated feelings. A mapper of fathomless psychological depth, a voyager in language, he was a man very much of his time and place yet universal and timeless in his sensibility.

Needless to say, he also had strong local connections. Oxford was on the direct carriageway from Stratford to London, and we can reasonably assume that he would have been a frequent visitor. In later years, when his fame was established, we know for a fact that Shakespeare became a good friend of Oxford's future mayor, John Davenant (and his notably attractive wife, Jane).

Davenant was a wealthy vintner who kept a tavern, later called The Crown, and it was on this site in 1927, at Number 3 Cornmarket, that the so-called 'painted room' was discovered, its wall paintings dating back to Shakespeare's time. Murals which had hitherto been covered by seventeenth-century oak panels, thick layers of Victorian canvas and modern wallpaper, were exposed. Might this have been the very room in which Shakespeare stayed on his travels? We can't know for certain.

We can, however, cross the road to the remains of St Martin's Church, Carfax. There sat the font (subsequently moved to St Michael at the Northgate, where it can still be seen) at which the Davenants' second son, William, was baptised on 3 March 1606. And there, beside it, once stood the baby's godfather, their close friend Mr Shakespeare.

The Bard's inspiring presence must have had some effect, for the boy went on to become Poet Laureate in 1638. (There were rumours that he may even have been his godfather's son.) So much is speculation; but of one thing we may be sure. William Shakespeare (like his First Folio which now resides in the Bodleian Library) was most definitely here.[22]

11

Seventeenth Century

SATURDAY, 30 JANUARY 1649. Was there ever a more dramatic day in the life of our nation? The execution of Charles I marks a profound moment in the constitutional history of this island, a statement in blood about the nature of authority, sovereignty and the law: an unforgettable public declaration of the basis for a justly governed society.

Why didn't Oliver Cromwell and the other signatories to the King's death warrant have Charles quietly murdered like so many of his royal predecessors? Why go to all the trouble of capturing him, recapturing him, imprisoning him in Carisbrooke castle on the Isle of Wight, putting him on trial in Westminster Hall – the very heart of Government – and going through a legal process to find him guilty? Why then decapitate him on a specially erected scaffold outside Whitehall Palace, for all to see?

That was the very point. In Cromwell's view justice had to be seen to be administered properly if the King were to be proven guilty of being 'a tyrant, traitor, murderer, and public enemy to the good people of this nation' with blood on his hands for having brought about the Civil War with all its devastating consequences for people up and down the land.

Once again Oxford was at the heart of the story. Charles, feeling unsafe in London where he faced Parliamentarian opposition and the ever-present danger of the mob, made Oxford his capital for more or less (from 29 October 1642 until 24 June 1646) the duration of the war.

Christ Church became the King's headquarters: Parliament was convened in its Great Hall. The Queen and her retinue were housed at Merton College. Prince Rupert and the royal children made St John's their base. The Schools of the Bodleian became storehouses and workshops. New College was transformed into a munitions warehouse. The mill at Osney was set to work grinding gunpowder rather than flour. New Inn Hall became the Royal Mint (much silver college plate was requisitioned and melted down to provide coinage). A gibbet was set up in Carfax. For more than three years Oxford's streets were filled with the clamour of courtiers, soldiers, horses and alarums as the royal entourage came and went.

One historian describes the bustling scene:

> Never was the city so crowded with grandees, important persons in state and church and army, with envoys and commissioners engaged in negotiations. Since it was the residence of the court there were the king's ministers and royal officials; the royalist Parliament met here, a majority of the Lords with perhaps a third of the Commons. Then there was the usual penumbra of a court, the hangers-on, the naughty ladies and dissolute men, the duellists and gamesters, poets and playwrights and journalists (a new profession). And at least two men of genius: Clarendon to write it all down in his *History*, and William Dobson, the first of English painters to date, who painted their portraits, in which we can still see the mingled strain and bravery of it all, the brief brilliance and sombre tragedy.[23]

There are remarkably few traces of the Civil War in Oxford today. The town was besieged three times but, mercifully, never slighted. The defensive ramparts and embankments which were constructed around it, so clearly visible on maps and paintings of the time, have long since melted into the ground (leaving only one remnant, in the garden of Rhodes House). In a corner of Port Meadow there is an area known as King Charles's racecourse, where he and

Prince Rupert continued their equestrian sport. The statue of the Virgin and Child above the porch of the University church bears the mark of passing Parliamentarian bullets. Outside Oxford there is, in the village of Old Marston, a dwelling known as Cromwell's house (though in fact it was the operational base for General Sir Thomas Fairfax). And the Civil War story is contained in the naming of North and South Parade, one supposedly marking the northernmost position of the Royalist forces, the other the southernmost deployment of the Parliamentary troops. These few signs apart, there is little to which one can point, which is extraordinary given the scale of devastation in other parts of the country.

Oxford University – if not always Oxford town – maintained its royal allegiance throughout the time of the Protectorate: the eleven-year national experiment with Cromwellian republicanism which followed Charles's execution. When the monarchy was eventually restored in 1660, Oxford underwent considerable rebuilding and investment. The Clarendon building, designed by Nicholas Hawksmoor and named in honour of Edward Hyde, Earl of Clarendon, King Charles II's most senior minister (and Chancellor of the University as well as Lord High Chancellor of the entire land) stands to this day as a monument to his power and prestige. It also reflects his popularity as a writer, for Clarendon's *History of the Great Rebellion and Civil Wars* is reputed to have sold so many copies that its royalties (no pun intended) were sufficient to fund the building in which was eventually housed the University Press.

The adjacent Sheldonian Theatre was begun in 1663 as the ceremonial centrepiece for the University, the place where degrees were conferred and distinguished visitors invited. It was built to the design of a promising young architect by the name of Christopher Wren, the precocious Savilian Professor of Astronomy at the University, who went on to reshape so much of London after the great fire of 1666.

Mention of Wren reminds us that the Sheldonian also stands next to what is now the History of Science Museum (then the site of the original Ashmolean), for science flourished in Restoration England. It was here that Professor John Wallis first introduced the infinity symbol ∞ in his *Mathesis Universalis* (1657). He was one of an exceptionally brilliant group of scholars who went on to form the nucleus of the Royal Society, two of whose greatest luminaries, Robert Hooke and Robert Boyle, used to meet to discuss their latest theories over a cup of the fashionably exotic New World beverage known as coffee, in what claims to be the oldest coffee house in England.[24] Another distinction for Oxford, and a soothing thought on which to end a century which, in the words of a popular 1640s ballad, had witnessed 'the world turned upside down'.

12

Eighteenth Century

It is remarkable that the quiet and remote county of Shropshire should have been the epicentre of a technological and industrial revolution – a revolution which was to transform Britain, and in due course the world. For it was here that an iron manufacturer, who had workshops and furnaces near a narrow gorge on the River Severn, found a way of heating metal to such a high temperature that he could produce iron which was both very strong and very light – making it a superb building material. His name was Abraham Darby. His grandson, also of that name, took the idea further and showed that it was possible to construct a bridge entirely of iron, big enough to span the gorge itself.

Ironbridge: the place is named after its greatest invention. Made from 379 tons of the revolutionary new metal, it was formally opened on New Year's Day 1781. People rushed to marvel at this wonder of the modern world; and they have been visiting ever since.

Nowhere in Britain was untouched by the new technology – and Oxford, as ever, made its own distinctive contribution. To supply fuel for the furnaces and transport the goods of the new industries a nationwide canal network was necessary – and one of its most important branches spurred off from the Grand Union through Oxford. For a decade it became the main artery between the Midlands and London. Tons of coal came down these waters, and much else besides. Wharves sprung up along its edges. Their remains can still be conjured up at Juxon Street, Walton Street and Hayfield Road. Here were unloaded goods to feed the colleges, warm their grates, and power the burgeoning city. And here, in the early years of the following century, Oxford's own Eagle Ironworks was established (better known as Lucy's after its Victorian owner, William Lucy). Production finally ceased as recently as 2005.

In parallel with the revolution in technology and manufacturing came a revolution in science and engineering. Historians have seen this as an Age of Enlightenment, an era when speculation about the supernatural gave way to exploration of the natural, a time when the phenomena of the material world were subjected to intense scrutiny, measurement, and experimental manipulation.

Not just on Earth – but in the heavens above. An

Observatory was built in Oxford in 1772 (completed in 1794) the second in the country after the Royal Observatory at Greenwich. Its chief architect was James Wyatt, and its distinctive octagonal design was based on the ancient Tower of the Winds which once stood in the agora of Classical Athens. It remains one of Oxford's most beautiful and distinctive buildings, recently fronted by a statue of Dr John Radcliffe, personal physician to the King and public philanthropist to the University, after whom both the 'Rad Cam' reading room and the 'JR' hospital take their name.

The skies above Oxford also witnessed a pioneering experiment in human flight. Early on the morning of 4 October 1784 James Sadler, a 31-year-old pastry chef, took off from Merton Field in a hot-air balloon fifty metres in circumference. He came back down to earth some six miles away, having ascended an estimated 3,600 feet and written himself into the record books as England's first aeronaut.

Academic standards within the University were somewhat less elevated than we might imagine in this apparently enlightened era. The poet Robert Southey wrote that he learnt only two things as an undergraduate at Balliol College: to row and to swim. Two more skills than Edward Gibbon acquired it would seem: the great historian spent a year at Magdalen

College in 1752 and thought his time there 'the most idle and unprofitable of my entire life', confessing to 'improprieties of conduct, ill-chosen company, late hours and inconsiderate expense'.

13

Nineteenth Century

THE INDUSTRIAL REVOLUTION moved a long way from its birthplace. It did so on wheels, along metal tracks, driven by engines powered by steam. Not quite as quickly as a rocket, but that is how it might have seemed 200 years ago, and that was the name given to the most famous locomotive ever built.

In the space of just a few years Britain was transformed – and with it the world. The great engineer, Isambard Kingdom Brunel, oversaw the building of a railway line called the Great Western which made it possible to travel from London to Bristol in a matter of hours rather than days. And from Temple Meads station in Bristol it was easy to connect with *SS Great Britain*, by far the largest ship in the world, built entirely from metal, propelled by steam and designed to cross the Atlantic Ocean to America, from where the 'Iron Horse' was to transform the face of that mighty continent.

The railway revolution nearly bypassed Oxford. Some University dons had shares in the Oxford Canal and were reluctant to see their investment diluted by competition. Others perceived a danger of moral contamination by accelerated proximity to the teeming metropolis of London. So they blocked plans to build a series of workshops, depots and sidings on the meadows nearby, leaving Didcot to become the main railway hub for the region.

There was one form of communication, however, in which Oxford continued to specialise and excel: the written word. In 1857 work began on the Oxford English Dictionary, one of the greatest works of collective scholarship ever undertaken, a monument to Victorian ambition and self-confidence. Overseeing this Herculean project was James Augustus Henry Murray, the self-educated son of a Scottish clothier. In the garden of his large, red-brick villa on the Banbury Road, he erected a corrugated iron outbuilding, lined with wooden shelves and pigeonholes, which he called his *scriptorium.* In it he filed over one million slips of paper on which were written quotations sent in from all over the globe following *An Appeal to the English-speaking and English-reading public.*

The English language remains our most successful and enduring export, and its spread was secured in tandem with the extraordinary expansion of the British Empire. By the end of the nineteenth century Victoria was no longer simply queen of an archipelago in the North Sea; she was Empress of the Indian subcontinent and head of state for millions of people across the entire planet. At its height it is said that a quarter of the map of the world was coloured imperial pink.

Great museums – the Natural History Museum, the Science Museum, the Victoria and Albert Museum – were established to curate and display the treasures garnered overseas. A Crystal Palace containing nearly a million square feet of glass was built in 1851 and in it a Great Exhibition was held. Another set of massive glasshouses was constructed at Kew in which plants from all over the planet could be grown and displayed. It still houses the world's largest collection of living plants – over thirty thousand different varieties – as well as seven million preserved specimens.[25]

Oxford already boasted the earliest botanical garden in the country (founded in 1621) and the earliest museum (1683). The Ashmolean was bulging with so many artefacts that it had to relocate to a bigger site on Beaumont Street in 1841. Also erected at around this time was the University Museum (housing a fine collection of rocks, dinosaur bones, and a mummified Dodo) to which was added in 1881 an Annexe, displaying a myriad extraordinary objects collected by the prodigious Augustus Henry Lane-Fox Pitt Rivers (1827–1900). A lieutenant-general in the Grenadier Guards, he was also a passionate archaeologist and ethnologist. With the superabundant energy which seems to have characterised so many Victorians he assembled over 20,000 artefacts from all over the world and arrange them typologically, according to use. His aim was to demonstrate the evolution of craft technologies in different places over different periods of time, thereby highlighting geographical, historical and cultural variation and adaptation. The number of items has now grown to nearly half a million, including a totem pole over eleven metres high, a witch in a stoppered bottle of silver glass, and, most famously, a collection of shrunken heads or *tsantas* made by the peoples of the upper Amazon. It remains one of the world's most extraordinary collections.

There was much other building development in Oxford during this period. The University Press moved to spacious premises on Walton Street in 1830. The entire massive Victorian suburb of North Oxford was constructed at this time, and several colleges came into being: Lady Margaret Hall (1878), Somerville (1879), St Hugh's (1886), St Hilda's (1893), and – spectacularly and controversially – Keble College (1868). Its extraordinary, multi-coloured brickwork arguably denotes the high-water mark of Victorian architectural ambition (and, in the view of some critics, bad taste) in Oxford.

The religious scene in Oxford was, as ever, complicated and contested. There was a flourishing of small, nonconformist chapels in working-class areas, and a large Methodist church was built in New Inn Hall Street (Oxford was, after all, intellectual home to the founder of Methodism, John Wesley). At the same time Oxford witnessed a resurgence in High Anglicanism, so closely associated with the university that it became known as the Oxford Movement and eventually even produced a cardinal (now saint), John Henry Newman of Trinity College.[26] Meanwhile, a pinnacled monument to the Oxford Martyrs was erected in prime position at the end of St Giles – as an unmissable reminder to Roman- and Anglo-Catholic parishioners of Oxford's determinedly Protestant heritage.

Atheism, too, became defensible in certain quarters. In 1811 Percy Bysshe Shelley had been sent down from University College for writing a pamphlet on *The Necessity of Atheism*, but by the mid-century it was much less shocking to promulgate god-denying beliefs. Oxford witnessed a key moment in the ideological history of the world. It was here, at the University Museum on 30 June 1860, that the scientist Thomas Henry Huxley and the Bishop of Oxford, Samuel Wilberforce, clashed over the implications of Charles Darwin's recently published *Origin of Species*, in the celebrated 'Apes versus Angels' evolution debate.

Change was all around, an 'overwhelming tide of change' in the words of one historian;[27] and no change was greater than in the arena of education. The 1854 University act made it permissible for students who were not from the Established Church to study at the highest level. In 1879 the first women were admitted to Oxford, though they were not formally allowed to take degrees until 1920 (two years after some of them had received the vote) and it was many years before gender parity was achieved. A law was introduced in 1870 providing school education for every child in the land aged from five to twelve – girls as well as boys. And, for the first time, other universities were founded in England, finally breaking Oxbridge's domination of higher education. 'We must', MP Robert Lowe commented after the extension of the franchise following the Second Reform Act of 1867, 'educate our masters.' The process had begun ...

14

Twentieth Century

BLUT UND EISEN was how Prussia came to dominate Germany according to its 'Iron Chancellor' Otto von Bismarck. If the nineteenth century was an age of iron, the twentieth could certainly be termed a century of blood.

It is estimated that seventeen million victims (military and civilian) died in the Great War that engulfed Europe from 1914 to 1918. Over *seventy* million died in the Second World War that followed two decades later. Britain lost a combined total of more than a million of her people in the mayhem. In nearly every town and village (and in nearly every Oxford college) there stands a plaque or well-tended war memorial inscribed with the names of the young men who marched off to war, never to return.

It is very curious that Oxford was never bombed, especially since the *Luftwaffe* attacked targets nearby – nearly 4,000 bombs fell on the county during the war. There is a theory that Hitler wanted the city as his future capital, or at least communication centre, in conjunction with Blenheim Palace.

Oxford's outstanding contribution to the war effort was in the field of intelligence. Bletchley Park was less than an hour away by train and it was there that the infamous German Enigma code was cracked by some of the finest minds in the country (though it has to be noted that Alan Turing, Gordon Welchman and Bill Tutte were all Cambridge graduates).[28]

When victory was eventually secured, the new Labour government under Clement Attlee (one of twenty-eight UK prime ministers to have graduated from Oxford) brought in wholesale reform, declaring a domestic war on the 'five giant evils' of want, disease, ignorance, squalor and idleness. Of all these reforms it was the creation in 1948 of a National Health Service, free at the point of use, which has proved the most celebrated. Spending on health almost doubled under the Attlee government. In the first year of its operation over five million pairs of spectacles were dispensed free of charge, some indication of the scale of the need which had hitherto gone unmet.

In tandem with reform of health provision came a major breakthrough in medical research. Blood was involved once again – this time for a benign purpose. And Oxford was, as ever, at the forefront of developments.

Alexander Fleming is credited with the discovery of penicillin in 1928; but he was never able to work out a way of producing it in sufficient quantity to make it a significant health benefit. For that we have to thank Howard Florey, a Rhodes scholar from Australia who later became Professor of Pathology (and Provost of The Queen's College).

At the Oxford Dunn School of Pathology Florey put together a research team of remarkably talented biochemists. Under his supervision the first ever clinical trial of penicillin was conducted in 1941 in the Radcliffe Infirmary. By the time Florey died in 1968 it is estimated that the antibiotic had saved over 200 million lives. (Fleming and Florey shared the Nobel Prize for medicine in 1945, together with the Oxford biochemist Ernst Chain.)

It fell to Dorothy Hodgkin, the only British woman scientist to have been awarded a Nobel Prize (in 1964), to confirm the precise chemical structure of penicillin through her pioneering X-ray crystallographic studies of biomolecules. (In 1969, after 35 years of research, Hodgkin also deciphered the structure of insulin.) One of her chemistry students at Somerville College in the 1940s was a young woman from Lincolnshire by the name of Margaret Roberts, who went on to become the UK's first female prime minister. Mrs Thatcher installed a portrait of her former tutor in 10 Downing Street – even though Hodgkin was a staunch Labour supporter.

At around the same time as Florey was developing his clinical work on penicillin, countless lives were being saved by another Oxford collaboration. The Oxford Committee for Famine Relief (Oxfam for short) was formed in 1942 with the aim of supporting the people of Greece, starving under Nazi occupation. Other campaigns followed. The first Oxfam shop opened at 17 Broad Street on 9 November 1949. Oxfam is now one of the world's largest aid organisations, with over 5,000 employees around the world, four times that number of volunteers, and a budget running into the hundreds of millions. Its headquarters remain in Oxford, less than five miles from where it first started.

Mass mobilisation, mass unemployment, mass consumption, mass media, mass communication, mass killing: the twentieth century was the century of the masses. The airwaves were filled by the telephone, the radio, the television, the personal computer and then the world wide web (founded in 1989 by Sir Tim Berners-Lee, a graduate of Queen's); while the physical landscape was transformed by the most influential force of the age – the motor car. And here, of course, Oxford had another remarkable contribution to make.

When William Morris sold his cycle business and used the proceeds to purchase a prime-site garage and workshop on Longwall Street, one local newspaper dubbed it 'The Oxford Motor Palace'. It was here, on 28 March 1913, that a car was built which was to change the course of history. Its name – could it really have been called anything else? – was the Morris Oxford; its badge an ox, fording the Isis.

The Morris Minor followed in 1928, by which point Morris Motors made up nearly 40 per cent of UK car production. By the time the MG Midget appeared, cars were being mass-produced at a rate of a thousand a week from vast premises on a disused military-school site in the nearby village of Cowley. Other factories followed, in Abingdon, Birmingham and Swindon, but Cowley was always heart of the Morris motor empire. At its peak 30,000 people were employed there, clocking on and off in vast droves, and changing forever the identity of the city down the road. The balance between town and gown shifted to the point where one wit talked of 'the city of screaming tyres' and another referred to Oxford as 'Cowley's Latin Quarter'.[29]

Morris changed the face of Oxford, and the Morris Oxford changed the face of Britain.

15

Twenty-First Century

THE SECOND MILLENNIUM dawned with the unforgettable image of New York's Twin Towers collapsing in flames. The horror of 9/11, caught on bystanders' camera-phones and beamed endlessly into living rooms around the world, heralded not only a new chapter in international relations, but also a revolution in the mode, speed and scale of global communication.

In 2018 the number of active Facebook users surpassed two billion. Instagram, which was only founded in 2010, exceeded one billion. The iPhone, first unveiled in 2007, enabled Apple to become the first technology business in the world to have a trillion-dollar valuation. Amazon, Microsoft, Google and Facebook follow close behind. It is also notable that nine of the top twenty global tech companies are Chinese.

Oxford is one of the UK's premier technology hubs. The commercial arm of the University, Oxford

University Innovation, launched no fewer than 24 high-tech firms in 2016. Investment in these spin-out companies now stands at over £500 million. And there are several other significant tech businesses in Oxford and its environs not directly related to the University. The Harwell Science and Innovation Campus, a few miles south of the city, is home to 200 organisations and companies, employing more than 5,000 staff.

In other twenty-first-century developments, a large mosque opened on Manzil Way, reflecting the rise of the Muslim population in East Oxford. The University expanded. We should say *both* universities expanded, for Oxford Polytechnic became Oxford Brookes University in 1992 and currently enrols fifty per cent more undergraduates (18,000 compared with 12,000[30]) than its senior neighbour down the hill. New centres like the Saïd Business School (2002) and the Blavatnik School of Government (2012) were created, and there was a surge of building throughout the University, including a major development of the old Radcliffe Infirmary site. Many of the new structures were architecturally distinguished and won awards. One or two – the abomination of Castle Mill in particular – were shockingly banal and unpopular.

Oxford United FC moved from the Manor Ground to the Kassam Stadium. A new railway line to London was opened at Oxford Parkway. The Westgate carpark was torn down and replaced with a new retail centre. Lucy's closed the Eagle Ironworks and, also in 2005, MG – the last remnant of the British motor manufacturing empire that once had Morris and Cowley at its heart – went into administration (its assets and brand purchased by Nanjing Automobile Group). The University's first female Vice Chancellor was appointed in 2016 – just as the last Oxford college finally went co-ed.

* * *

This book is being written in the wake of a lunar landing – nearly fifty years to the day after Apollo 11 touched down on the Sea of Tranquillity in 1969. The unmanned spacecraft which made its landing (this time on the far side of the moon) was launched from China, confirming that country's status as a superpower to rival America. Oxford now educates over 1,300 Chinese students and employs 240 Chinese members of staff, most of whom are based in the large and impressive China Centre on Canterbury Road which opened in 2014. Meanwhile, Oxford City Council has signed a memorandum of understanding with Langfang City People's Government and Hebei Province to 'promote further cooperation', and St

Giles is routinely filled with coaches dropping off Chinese tourists, something unseen two, let alone five, decades ago.

Also established in Oxford in recent times is the Future of Humanity Institute (2005). Its declared mission is to develop

> ... big picture research focus(ing) on the planet-term consequences of our actions today, and the complicated dynamics that are bound to shape our future in significant ways. A key aspect to this is the study of existential risks – events that endanger the survival of Earth-originating, intelligent life or that threaten to drastically and permanently destroy our potential for realising a valuable future.

Who knows what prognostications it will make, or how the history of Oxford in the twenty-first century will be written in years to come?

An oblique clue is perhaps offered by another contemporary structure. One of the smallest and least-known Oxford colleges is the strangely named Harris Manchester. In 2014, with funding from two Thai benefactors, a new building was opened – an entrance portico and, adjoining it, an octagonal bell-tower. There is nothing modern about the architectural vision, and nothing digital about the clock-face which adorns it. This is old-fashioned architecture achieved in the most up-to-date way, topped off by a copper weathervane featuring a book-bearing Oxford don on a bicycle, in a mortar board and gown.

On the tower is an inscription attributed to Dorothy L. Sayers (born in Oxford and a graduate of Somerville College):

It's later than you think.
But it's never too late.

It was chosen in recognition of the college's population of mature students (you have to be aged over 21 to study there). In similar vein, the bell peals at two minutes past the hour.

Oxford has always hovered on the edge of time, at once curiously arcane and fustily traditional, yet seemingly able to foster pioneering research and cutting-edge innovation. The university has never stood still; it has always evolved. 'Institutions have waxed and waned over the centuries but Oxford has always succeeded in reinventing itself to meet the demands of a new age.'[31]

16

Once and Future

AH YES. NEARLY FORGOT. That other person we mentioned. The mystery figure in the castle ...

He turns out to be none other than the most famous monarch in British history: our once and future king, King Arthur.

Arthur wasn't conceived in Tintagel Castle as some would have us believe. Arthur was conceived in Oxford. For Arthur was a character in a work of the imagination. Its title was *The History of the Kings of Britain* (*Historia Regum Britanniae*) and it was written in Oxford – within the walls of Oxford Castle to be precise.

That was where the Chapel of St George was located. And it is where a cleric called Geoffrey of Monmouth was based from 1129 to 1151. In its heyday St George's was a flourishing centre for learning, supporting a community of clergy and students. Alongside his work as canon to the Chapel, and in tandem with his role as *magister* or teacher, Geoffrey penned a number of works, the most celebrated of which was the *History.*

It is a sweeping narrative of royal rule across several centuries. Also playing their part in the story are Arthur's father Uther Pendragon, his counsellor and magus, Merlin (whose *Life* and *Prophecies* Geoffrey also 'recorded'), his wife Guinevere, and his sword Excalibur. The epic ends with his tragic defeat by Mordred at the battle of Camlann, and his journey to a place of final rest at Avalon.

Geoffrey staunchly maintained that his work was a direct translation from an ancient book in Welsh, originally from Brittany, supplied to him by Walter, Archdeacon of Oxford – a statement which, according to one scholar, is 'about as plausible as Tolkien claiming the Lord of the Rings was written by Hobbits'.[32]

Whatever its origin, the *History* was an instant hit. 'Geoffrey's was a brilliant concoction, providing the post-Conquest kings of England with a history as bogus, as rich, as colourful and as downright entertaining as Virgil had provided for the Emperor Augustus.'[33] Its influence on the medieval imagination cannot be overstated. It rapidly became one of the most important and popular histories in world literature. 'Altogether it is astonishing what that single work coming out from the shadows of the tower of Oxford Castle achieved.'[34]

St George's Chapel no longer stands. It was demolished to make way for the expanding castle. All that remains is the underground crypt, dark, candlelit, mysterious.

As for Arthur, he lives on to this day. His association with our venerable city seems to epitomise Oxford's curious combination of scholarship, antiquity, eccentricity and legend. Magical. Strangely timeless. Once and future.

* * *

Notes

1 No one knows quite why it was so called. The speculation is that it is an abbreviation of the Latin *Thamesis.*

2 There is some debate about the precise location of the 'original' fording place, the main contenders being a western route via North Hinksey, and the extant crossing at Folly Bridge. No one knows for sure, and it may well have changed over time. As to the name, the first formal record of the name 'Oxford' (*Oxnaforda*) is in the *Anglo-Saxon Chronicle* (912).

3 Oxford city centre is known as Carfax (a corruption of the Norman 'quatre vois' or 'four ways': in other words the crossroads between the four gates to the ancient walled town.

4 The street pattern seems likely to have been finalised during the reign of Alfred's son, Edward the Elder (899–924).

5 For a map of the Danelaw, showing its proximity to Wessex and suggesting the pivotal role Oxford must have played as a frontier trading down and defensive settlement, see: https://en.wikipedia.org/wiki/Danelaw#/media/File:England_878.svg

6 One of Aethelred's other sons, Edmund II (known as 'Ironside') is thought to have been crowned at Oxford in 1016 (and possibly murdered here too). At a *Witan*, or Assembly of Elders, held in Oxford two decades later (1035) one of Sweyn's grandsons, Harold 'Harefoot', was made King, thus confirming Oxford's importance in national affairs at this time.

7 Recent archaeology suggests that d'Oilly incorporated pre-existing defences into the new building, and that St George's Tower is of Saxon origin.

8 Chaucer also wrote (in 1391) a scientific treatise on the astrolabe, using a measurement of latitude based on Oxford. Oxford at this time seems to have had 'a reputation as a kind

of mediaeval Greenwich', according to A.L. Rowse, *Oxford in the History of the Nation* (Weidenfeld, 1975) p.34.

9 Rowse, p.10.

10 Robert of Cricklade's great work was *Defloratio historie naturalis Plinii*, an abridgement of Pliny the Elder's magisterial *Natural History*.

11 One Archdeacon in particular – Walter of Oxford (d.1151). See Chapter 16.

12 'Unworkable' is the verdict of A.L. Rowse: 'We must remember that these people running the country, king and magnates alike, were Frenchmen.' Rowse, p.41.

13 Michael De-la-Noy, *Exploring Oxford* (Headline, 1991) p.14.

14 W.A. Pantin, *Oxford Life in Oxford Archives* (Oxford, 1972) p.9.

15 Pantin, p.75.

16 The story of the 'Stamford Secession' and its supposed link to the door knocker of Brasenose college is very thoroughly told here: http://stamfordlocalhistorysociety.org.uk/brazenose-site-stamford

17 H. Rashdall, in F.M. Powicke and A.B. Emden (eds) *The Universities of Europe in the Middle Ages* (Oxford, 1936) (iii) p.96, quoted in Pantin, p.68.

18 Geoffrey Tyack, *Oxford: An Architectural Guide* (Oxford, 1998) p.49.

19 Tyack, p.39.

20 Rowse, p.56.

21 As an aside, the legendary buccaneer Sir Henry Morgan (1635–1688) had a flagship called *Oxford*. It sank off the coast of Haiti in 1669, with the loss of much booty and over 200 men, when a spark from a pig roast aboard deck ignited the powder magazine. Morgan was blown into the water by the force of the explosion, but survived.

22 Those who argue that Shakespeare could not possibly have written the works ascribed to him, point instead to Edward de Vere, seventeenth Earl of Oxford as the real author – the so-called 'Oxfordian theory'.

23 Rowse, p.93.

24 The Grand Café claims to be on the *site* of the nation's first coffee house. The Queens Lane Café (opposite) claims to be the oldest *continuously operating* coffee house.

25 Oxford's Rewley Road station, opened in 1851, was a cast-iron prefabricated structure, created by the same contractor who had built the Crystal Palace. The station was dismantled when the Saïd Business school was built, and moved to a museum in Buckinghamshire.

26 Canonised in 2019.

27 Ian Mortimer, *Millennium: From Religion to Revolution: How Civilization Has Changed Over a Thousand Years* (Pegasus, 2016) p.258.

28 As, incidentally, were all three 'Oxford Martyrs'.

29 Pantin, p.104.

30 The ancient university has an additional 12,000 graduate students – i.e. the same number as undergraduates.

31 Laurence Brockliss, *The University of Oxford: A Brief History* (Bodleian Library, 2019, p.7).

32 Nick Higham, *King Arthur* (The History Press, 2015) p.79.

33 Higham, p.83.

34 Rowse, p.17.

Appendix

The Origins of the University

THE ENTITY WE refer to as Oxford University evolved over many centuries in an organic, often haphazard, and sometimes downright bewildering way, which is part of its idiosyncratic fascination – and frustration. This is a brief attempt to trace its early history.

In the beginning there was no 'university'. The way it all started was that men of learning ('masters') would lease premises from Oxford landlords, then invite students to enrol to hear them lecture: they were freelance tutors seeking paying pupils if you like. There were five main subject areas: arts (rhetoric and philosophy), theology, canon law, civil law and medicine.

The students would be accommodated in various lodging houses and hostels dotted around the town. Naturally, they tended to board with others from their place of origin. So the dwellings took on a particular character and personality. A motley collection of academic 'halls' grew up, forerunners of today's colleges.

In so far as there was a nucleus or common meeting place, it was the church of St Mary the Virgin, located centrally but far enough away from the bustle of Carfax to enable studious contemplation and debate. Different parts of the church provided a venue for different faculties and purposes. Sessions of the university court were held in the Lady Chapel. Decision-making by the entire convocation (the collective name for the assembly of masters) took place in the chancel. And, adjoining the church, in 1190, a stone 'school' or *scholia* was built where students ('scholars') could gather to attend lectures and exchange ideas with their masters.

A support network of parchment makers, book-binders and illuminators grew up in nearby Catte Street and before long a kind of academic proto-industry had been spawned. Indeed, the model on which the academics organised themselves was that of industry at the time, with bachelors and masters of arts being comparable to apprentices and master craftsman in the guilds.

Like guilds, these educational communities were self-financing and proudly autonomous. They organised themselves under a Head of House and remained determinedly independent except in so far as they formed a loose federation or *universitas*, headed by a Chancellor. Robert Grosseteste (1175–1253) scholar, theologian, scientist and later Bishop of Lincoln (Oxford was in the diocese of Lincoln at this time) is credited with being one of the university's first and most distinguished Chancellors, or 'Master of the Scholars' (*magister scolarum*) as he was termed – though precisely what practical powers he had is unclear.

As time went on, investment in education became more focused. Money was injected in the form of patronage from rich and powerful private benefactors. They provided funds for the establishment of what came to be called Colleges. These were fixed properties, built for posterity, owned outright rather than leased, with endowments, assets in land and livestock, statutes of incorporation, codes of conduct, and a self-governing body of 'Fellows'. William of Durham endowed University College in 1249. John Balliol, father of a future King of Scots, founded the college which bears his name. Walter de Merton, Lord Chancellor of England, did likewise. (These are unanimously acknowledged to be the three earliest colleges, though in typical Oxford fashion there is considerable disagreement about which came first.)

The tradition of proud independence, self-regulation and distinctive diversity was reinforced rather than diluted under the college system. The heads of colleges (elected by the Fellowship) consciously took on different titles – President, Principal, Provost, Rector, Warden, Dean, Master (it was many hundreds of years before there was to be a Mistress) – as if to underline this sense of separate personality.

To this day a student's primary allegiance is to their college rather than to the university, which is viewed as a rather distant, somewhat nebulous and largely bureaucratic institution. W.A. Pantin's fascinating book, *Oxford Life in Oxford Archives,* (full of insights based on the records he meticulously organised from 1946 to 1969) draws attention to the fact that official university (i.e. centralised as opposed to individual college) records for the admission of undergraduates began in only 1565, more than three centuries after young men had first come to Oxford to study.

He also notes that although there were various attempts to try to make students attend at least one lecture every day, this proved difficult to enforce (to this day registers of attendance are viewed with suspicion). So the only accurate, quantifiable and, as he puts it, 'really stable unit of university discipline ... was not the lecture-room, but the place where a man eats and sleeps – the hall of residence' (Pantin, p.2).

In other words, even though the university preceded the colleges, responsibility for the welfare and discipline of undergraduates was, from the very outset, 'shifted from those who teach to those who provide board and lodging' – a principle which still holds in Oxford today. Pantin adds:

> The thing that makes the admissions system (if you can call it that) of modern Oxford so peculiarly complex, namely the placing of admissions in the hands of some thirty [as it was then, in 1972: it is now 39 plus six permanent private halls] independent and co-equal authorities, can really be traced back to the disciplinary problems of the Middle Ages, when it was found most effective to place the control and admission of undergraduates in the hands of the principals of the halls, and, later, of the colleges. (Pantin, p.3)

To make matters even more complicated, there were no formal university examinations or standardised entrance qualifications. (These weren't introduced until 1926.) This helps to explain the wide range of ages of admission. John Donne was twelve when he went up in 1584; his brother Henry a year younger. And one student is recorded as matriculating at the tender age of eight.

Bemused visitors to Oxford will search in vain

for a 'campus' or headquarters building. 'Where is the university?' they ask. It's a perfectly reasonable question, to which the only answer is a sympathetic shrug. There's a main library (the Bodleian), a main church (St Mary the Virgin), a main testing centre (the Examination Schools), and a ceremonial gathering place (the Sheldonian). Apart from that the buildings are organised according to college or subject of study. Few students know, still less care, where the 'University Administration and Services' department is (Wellington Square for the record, in a suitably faceless building).

A List of Oxford Colleges in Order of Foundation

University	1249
Balliol	1263
Merton	1264
Exeter	1314
Oriel	1326
Queen's	1341
New	1379
Lincoln	1427
All Souls	1438
Magdalen	1458
Brasenose	1509
Corpus Christi	1517
Christ Church	1546
Trinity	1555
St John's	1555
Jesus	1571
Wadham	1612
Pembroke	1624
Worcester	1714

Hertford	1740
Keble	1868
Lady Margaret Hall	1878
Somerville	1879
St Hugh's	1886
St Hilda's	1893
St Anne's	1952
St Antony's	1953
St Edmund Hall	1957
Nuffield	1958
St Peter's	1961
St Catherine's	1963
Linacre	1965
St Cross	1965
Wolfson	1966
Kellogg	1994
Mansfield	1995
Harris Manchester	1996
Green Templeton	2008
Reuben	2020

In some cases the term 'foundation' can be misleading, because it applies to a technical, legal process. Hence the dispute about which college is in fact the oldest (as opposed to the first to be formally 'founded'). There is also the question of Colleges being renamed. Thus Hertford College, which formally became a college in 1740, grew out of Hart Hall, whose origins stretched back into the thirteenth century. This is even more the case with St Edmund Hall (which still proudly refers to itself as a hall despite being accorded college status in a charter of incorporation of 1957). It takes its name from St Edmund of Abingdon, former Archbishop of Canterbury, who taught in a house on the site in the 1190s, and has a claim to be the oldest establishment to house and educate undergraduates continuously in any university anywhere in the world. Green College was founded in 1977 but renamed Green Templeton in 2008. Rewley House (1990) became Kellogg College in 1994. And so on ...

There are also six Permanent Private Halls, which have identical access to university facilities, but which are governed by Christian denominations rather than fellows, as with a college. These are: Blackfriars (Dominican), Campion Hall (Jesuit), Regent's Park (Baptist), St Benet's (Benedictine), St Stephen's (Anglo-Catholic) and Wycliffe Hall (Church of England, Evangelical). Blackfriars was originally founded, at a different site, in 1221.

Acknowledgements

Morris Oxford is fortunate indeed to have so many loyal, generous, and knowledgeable subscribers. Of these, two have been exceptionally helpful in reading various drafts of this book: Jack Holland and Stewart Richards. Our sincerest thanks to them, as to Merlin Matthews, Nick Allen and Nick Evans on the design front: a quite simply brilliant team.

Onward and Oxford!

About Morris Oxford

The strapline for the **Morris Oxford** website is *People, Places, Things - Stories from Oxford*; and that, we hope, just about sums it up. Every month a new story is posted on some aspect of our remarkable city. See for yourself - and if you have Oxford stories of your own, we'd love to hear from you.

www.morrisoxford.co.uk/feedback

Printed in Great Britain
by Amazon

47633484R00061